Some Sense of Transcendence

By the same author:

Of Earth, 1974
Invisibilities, 1977
Triptych, 1979
From Dream, From Circumstance:
New & Selected Poems, 1963-1983, 1984
Once Around Bullough's Pond, 1987

Some Sense of Transcendence

Poems

1983–1998

Douglas Worth

William L. Bauhan, Publisher
Dublin, New Hampshire

Library of Congress Cataloguing in Publication Data:
Worth, Douglas.
Some Sense of Transcendence :poems, 1983-1998 / Douglas Worth.
p. cm.
ISBN 0-97233 124-5 (alk. paper)
I. Title.
PS36573. 0696S65 1999
813' .54--dc21 99-18844
CIP

Printed in the United States of America

Contents

for Pat

Middle Age

Having somehow survived the traumas
of growing up, passing
from school into the world
of your first job, marriage, divorce, analysis
second marriage, suburbs, mortgages
womb terrors, deliveries, diapers
playgroups, Miss Von Krump at Nursery School

you arrive at an afternoon
when for the first time since what seems like forever
they've all disappeared, leaving you
on your own, for the moment, one somewhere off at a schoolmate's
the other up the street, and your wife working late

and after you've relished the quiet luxury
of having nothing immediate to do
spreading out around you for half-an-hour
you find that you're really not quite sure what to do
with yourself, and you suddenly picture your mother
when you'd get home from dances, sitting up alone
on the porch in darkness, her cigarette flaring, dying

so you shake yourself and go down
to the basement to dust off the piano
but the notes have gone stiff and sour
so you come back up
and take down some Dostoyevsky
you haven't looked at since college
but it's underlined, with notes
in your first wife's hand
so you put on an old favorite Beethoven sonata
but it's fuzzy and scratched and repeats
and repeats and repeats

and by now you're in no mood
to attack that set of exams
you should have done over the weekend
or tangle with the new poem
that seemed hopelessly snarled this morning

and so, for the moment, defeated, you just sit still
at a loss, alone, in the livingroom, drowning in silence
a bit scared, resentful and sorry for yourself
because here you are, after all those years
of responsible adulthood, having made it through
in one piece, if not exactly with flying colors
to middle age, and suddenly free at last
and nobody's handing out stars, or calling up
to ask if you can come out after dinner to play.

The Wicked Stepmother, Revisited

She seemed a good deal less monstrous, this time around—
granted that little curl to one side of her mouth
was not very nice, as she called her stepdaughter down
from her tower-room dream of the prince in his
neighboring castle
to add one more item to the impossible list
of tedious household chores the girl had to get done
before she could start getting ready to go to the ball.

Somehow, it was clear, Cindy'd get there anyway,
or, if she didn't, it wouldn't really matter—
she'd land her prince soon enough, with those heavenly eyes,
that pert little pout, crystal voice, lilting swing to her skirt
that already had all the local bluebirds and mice
scrambling after her and squabbling among themselves
over who got to bring her the sponge or help make up her bed.

Well, how would you have felt, up against all that,
with two girls from a previous marriage to look out for,
neither one with sufficient wit or grace or charm
to offset her lack of looks or inheritance,
and the constant suggestion, in that goody two-shoes,
of how wonderfully gifted, ingenuous, loving, bright
and beautiful your predecessor had been?

That would have been enough to sour a saint!
But then, just as she was easing over the hump
of middle age, to suddenly lose her husband—
and not for the first time, having hauled herself back
from that earlier blow, with a wound that had never healed
so much as scarred over, leaving a tightness inside
against which she'd fought to stay open, vulnerable.

After that echoing slam and sharp click, she'd turned
to take in the downhill slide of the rest of her life:
the endless evenings of staring into a fire
or nodding over a book, or trying to figure
how far the relentless cancer of inflation
had sapped her small income, gnawed at her modest savings,
with back payments piling and dowries looming ahead.

Small wonder, then, as the night of the ball approached,
if she lay awake, in a bed grown much too large
for herself and the cat, scheming how to keep Cinderella
back a bit longer, while, with a few deft waves,
choice sprinklings, and abracadabras of her own,
she did what she could to turn her two ugly ducklings
into swans with a chance to fly off with the prince's heart

as she, on a magical night, thirty years before,
lovely, in moonlight, as she could ever be,
had blossomed under his hands 'til they shook with desire
and his lips found the pulse at her throat and slid
down and down,
and for a few hours there was no such thing as the laundry,
the rent, or good sense, and her hand-me-down,
size-too-small slippers
were chalices, overflowing with champagne.

Old Wine

(for Dorrit)

You could have gone
sharp and sour, thinned
by loss after loss after loss,
alone in some dim
room full of musty
furniture, nodding off, dreaming
of distant, sunlit
hillsides, young laughter, strong arms
pulling you down . . .

instead you kept growing
deeper, more varied, open
to light and dark,
giving yourself
in rich sips and swigs away,
letting grief, as it aged you,
bring out the subtle
bouquet of all you had been
as daughter, wife, mother—precious
balm to the world.

Triptych

(in memoriam)

Passing On

(for Dad)

For a time

I couldn't see
a gull sweep down to break
the skin of a pond

or hear Fats or Garner
growling over the keys,
their fingers scattering reckless
fistfulls of notes

or recall
the last time I saw you
at 5 a.m. in the driveway of the shore cottage
as we pulled out:
hands flapping, jumping up and down
in your weathered khakis, mud-caked basketball sneakers,
beard waggling, making faces at the kids—
the "eminent naturalist," still a kid yourself
four months before cancer dragged you down
again, for the final time . . .

without some sting or ache
as of violation
brimming my throat and eyes,
as if you had been torn
from things you loved,

or your loss had somehow knocked them
out of focus,
their contours blurring, smudged
by death's rough thumb.

Now, more and more
white wings curve
immaculate
against blue

strewn notes flow clear
in lusty
joyfullness

my bearded, scrunched-up mug
wags at my kids

as you settle back in
to all you used to be
and, sharing, gave me to treasure,
become, pass on.

Bonds

(for Mother)

Unlikely candidate
for a husband's pyre,
you fell, cracking six ribs
within a month of Dad's death,
and a few weeks later,
before we'd had time

to catch our breaths, again,
were lying beside him, ashes
in the earth.

Loving parties as he loved nature and solitude,
bright queen of many a brilliant soiree,
witty and venemous,
with no focus to fulfill or make you happy
beyond such occasions
and wife and motherhood,
you lashed at him night after night
for fifty years,
yet never divorced
remarking, when you learned he had killed himself
after a nightmare year of pain and drugs,
"I'm glad for Brooke. I hope
he left half the pills,"
unable to believe, in those next few weeks
that he wasn't about
to knock at the door of your room
to take you to dinner.

And he, long-suffering
infuriatingly placid
saint that he was—
who could keep your sophisticated friends enthralled
for hours, detailing the sexlife of the earthworm—
confessed to me once, over twenty years ago,
driving me to the station after a visit,
when I dared to ask how he'd stood it all those years,
that he'd never stopped loving you.

In the motel parking lot,
the day before what was left of you was lowered
in a little fragrant sandalwood box you loved,

I heard a sudden commotion overhead
and, looking up, saw a couple
of Canada geese in tandem—
he leading, she close behind—
honking and stroking slowly across the sky.
They made me think, aside from the obvious
parallel to your deaths,
of the poem you stunned us by quoting
six weeks before, as we drove to bury Dad,
by the ancient Greek lyric poet, Callimachus,
in which he mourns the loss of a dear friend
with whom he'd so often "talked the sun down the sky."

Funny what you don't know
about people, lives.

It was Mike, the non-verbal one, supposedly,
of us three "kids,"
who stood up during the joint memorial service
and spoke so movingly
about how, despite everything
the two of you'd stuck together
through thick and thin

like those geese, I suppose,
who Val told us
bond for life.

And now you've gone to join him
in death as well,
releasing us from your anguish
into our lives
where we must learn to stop trying
to make you happy
who can never stop loving you.

Post Mortem

(for Val and Mike)

you go on
with the rest of your life

plunging back into work
conversing
fixing breakfast
shopping for groceries
courting the angel of sleep

surprised by how easy it is—
between moments of wavering landscapes,
lava scalding your throat—
to cope

impressed by how far you've managed
to come on your own
and are likely to continue
before it's your turn to follow

resolving
to savor each day
as precious, miraculous
failing

picking up gestures, phrases,
the arc of a smile,
and other fragments
of immortality
that glint out at you
from memories, photos, the telephone
mirrors, your kids

probing gently, pearling over
with regret
the lodged, indissoluble grit
of awful times

a bit numbed
as if some secret organ or limb
had been cut out, or gone to sleep
so that you find yourself missing
little familiar things:
verb tenses, your step:

saying "has always loved"
when "has" is no longer correct

climbing the stairs with the tray
of Saturday morning
newspaper, coffee, toast
without the juice

fumbling carkeys with mittens,
a bundle under one arm,
then suddenly down
on the hard, packed snow of the parking lot,
clutching your ribs, or an ankle, gingerly
checking what's left of the eggs.

Ascent

Leaving the autoroute we start to climb
through green into deeper green, winding up and around
rockface, the air, sweet with meadow, fresh with pine,
like the touch of someone who knows us well and loves us
despite everything, cool at our brows, gently wiping away
the film and grit of daily aggravations,
ambitions, failures, guilts, anxieties.

Halfway, as we stop to look out at the patchwork quilt
of farmland and forest sloping to snow-capped peaks,
the air by now so steeped in fragrances
we don't so much breathe as sip it, savoring,
a hidden bird closeby begins to spill
such rapture, swelling, on and on, we shiver
feeling it pierce us, gather, rise and brim.

Arriving, toward nightfall, time seems to have skipped some beats
as the familiar red-cheeked, smiling matron
greets us, the same earth-brown farmers drinking beer
crowd round their table, the same rich cooking smells
follow us up the stairway to our room
whose beds are piled high with fairy toadstool puffs
onto which we collapse with sighs of utter bliss.

Waking, after dreamless sleep, to the sound
of water rushing, we open all the windows
and lie back naked, skin silked with early light,
your breasts echoing the mountains framed in the distance;
for a moment the sense that things have been like this
for a long, long time—forever maybe—broken
as I reach out to touch you, name you, and you turn.

Breakfast out on the terrace, sunlight caressing
everything, dancing, shimmering, iridescent

swallows feeding on air, geraniums
outblazing the raspberry, cherry, red currant jams
we scoop and spread with sweet butter over the pure
white inner nests of rolls, pouring cup after cup
from steaming pitchers of coffee and hot frothed milk.

Walking for hours along a grassy ridge,
dwarfed by encircling peaks, words fall away
as our spirits, soaring, merge with the primal grandeur
of rock and sky—creation, emptiness;
calling us back, at our feet, the sprinkled notes
of blue and gold bells and stars embellishing
an ever-stretching symphony of green.

Evening, exhausted, drunk with Alpenglow,
wine and contentment, we stroll the quiet streets
of the village, gazing up at the scattered lights
of chalets in the high meadows, above them stars
in brightening patterns far beyond the scope
of Bear or Archer—infinite, bright hosts
locked endlessly in war or love with Darkness.

Coming back down, next morning, slowly, in second,
one foot on the brake, into gas fumes, a thickening haze
of remembered schedules, deadlines, debts, we swear
this time it will be different—somehow we'll keep,
shining inside us, shedding soft radiance
on those around us, something of the eternal
mysterious, holy unity of things.

We have, after all, that perfect pebble we found
sparkling at us as we knelt to drink, somewhere
in one of our bags, and how could we forget
that sudden songburst flooding us, or the moment
we turned to each other, your opening lips like rose
and honey mingling—the same lips telling me now,
sharply, to shift into third and watch the road!

Crucifixion

(attributed to Donatello, ca. 1450
San Piero a Sieve (Firenze)
Convento di Bosco ai Frati)

As opposed to the other
slim figures, heads drooping
sideways, limbs pinned, piteously
suspended, almost floating
upon the cross,
fresh trickles brightly streaking
the forehead, arms, and feet
of the noble, heroic
shell of the still unrisen
Son of God,

here hangs the naked body
of what, 'til a few minutes ago,
had been a skinny, short, plain-featured man,
vain of his close-cropped beard,
from whom the life has been drained slowly out—
the flesh not yet stinking,
dumbly straining, along with the bones,
to slump from the spikes
that skewer the no longer wriggling hands;
lids not quite closed over bulging orbs;
teeth clamped on the dry wafer
of the tongue;
chest and belly crosshatched
with clotted slits;
genitals shriveled;

one foot curled over the other,
the long toes splayed as if
in agony—

here hangs no chrysalis
but a dead man
in whom the spirit burned
to accomplish something
immense, profound, outrageous, radical
as turning hate and war to peace and love,
a spark that, flaming, caught, and, slowly, steadily,
ever more quickly widening, blazed and spread. . .

its bright source here
extinguished, openly, publicly
stamped out
by an alarmed, self-perpetuating world
which claims him now, waiting
to draw him down and back
to the dust from which
mysteriously, he rose.

Easter

Amid lavender
white, yellow
crocuses, jellybeans, eggs

we find bits of Jesus
blossoming
out of the dead

from the cracks
in our hearts, the moss-covered
stones of our heads.

Peace Maker

(for Daniel Berrigan)

Asked, for a change, to comment

not about pouring your blood
over nose cones, prisons, the Pentagon, Nicaragua
or other such obvious
places you'd recently been

but about what you thought
of Saint Francis of Assisi,

after what seemed an awkward
moment's shifting of gears:
dumbfoundment? bemusement? titters
rippling the crowd,

you mentioned a painting
given to you by an artist
dying of cancer

that portrayed the saint praying
one arm round his brother
wolf,
the latter looking ferocious
and none-too-well fed.

It made you wish
Saint Francis well,
you said,

and went on,
once the swell of uneasy amusement
at your cryptic understatement
had subsided,
to suggest that perhaps one measure
of a peace maker—
Gandhi, King, those
whose lives you have tried to live by—
is the tenacity
with which one is willing to bear
one's message, over and over,
down from some cherished mountain top
tower, porch, lecturn,
and speak it
into the slobbering fangs of aggression

feeling the hot, sour breath
ablaze in your nostrils,
flinging an arm round the bony neck,
kneeling to pray

not just for the ravenous
creature panting beside you,
but that other, waiting
to gobble you up
inside.

Bluebird Feather

dull gray
'til you hold it up
turn it
to the light
slowly
so

Athens, July, 1984

Things kept falling apart as we toured Athens:
the guidebook; one of my sandals; a paper bag
filled with peaches; a bedside lamp at the hotel;
Danny, sampling a rusk our first morning at breakfast;
Mommy, leaving her camera at a cafe;
Colin with stomach cramps; me with a case of the runs;
the sky itself, as far-hurling Zeus sent his bolts
and it rained for two days—unheard of in July.

We went up Mount Lycabettos nevertheless,
surveyed the sprawling city, its priceless treasures
being gnawed by a haze of smog; strolled gratefully
sucking popsicles along the shady paths
of the National Gardens; stuffed ourselves with museums
and monuments, climbing late one sweltering morning
with the crowds up the Acropolis to gaze
in frazzled wonder, jostling amidst the rubble,
at what had been civilization's masterpiece
of balance and harmony—ponderous stone caught up
in an effortless dance with space and shadow and light:
the Parthenon! whose crumbling magnificence
gaped back at us through a maze of scaffolding
like an aging goddess having some bridgework done.

From stumps, skewed pillars, scraps of pediment,
maimed figures missing limbs, heads, genitals,
we tried to resurrect the ancient glory
of Athens twenty-four centuries ago;
and some of the pieces—Poseidon poised to launch
his trident; Nike bending to her sandal;
a charging stallion—blazed as we stopped to stare.

But what seemed to me most alive in that city of ruins
and taxis spoke through my recurring sense
of something behind things: featureless, elusive,
spirit, urge, idea, manifesting itself
agelessly, inexhaustibly, in marble,
bronze, or the softer medium of flesh,
glimpsed here and there most purely: two translucent
swallowtails, delicate gold and black, whirling together
in flawless azure over the Parthenon;
three Naiads cooling their honey-colored limbs
at a fountain by a cafe where we had lunch;
a sun-bronzed Dionysus on a bus
in sawed-off jeans, who'd have kept Praxiteles
coaxing cold stone to ecstasy for weeks;
and the photo on a wall in our hotel bedroom
of a woman kneeling naked at tide's edge, foam
swirling around her thighs, who seemed to be
rising, night after night, from the womb of the sea.

Some Sense Of Transcendence

(Mexico, 1987)

1

Everything tilts, is sinking
back to mud.

One aisle of the great Spanish cathedral
in Mexico City's Zocalo lists crazily
from the plumb lines of the long-corded chandeliers,
floor tiles cracking, spewed up—you lose your sense
of balance, order, the vast house of God
lurching back to the ancient marshy island
of Aztec Tenochtitlan. A stone's throw from there,
half-excavated, the colossal
pyramid-temples, drenched with centuries
of sacrifice, skewed also, plunge drunkenly back
through layer on layer of conquest, rebellion, dust
toward some obscure, fresh, primal flowering.

2

Second, guarded glances of surprise
darting up from brown, dark-eyed, wide-mouthed faces
as we stand squished in the Metro, or I shoulder my way
through the market near the Zocalo, clutching both zippers
of my backpack, robbed once already . . . but those looks
mingling curiosity with something hostile, suspicious,
and something of intrigue—almost as if
this light-skinned, whiskered figure might be
not just another rich, loud gringo tourist
but Cortes, Christ, or, even, this time, the true
Quetzalcoatl: wise, kind, gentle teacher,

plumed serpent, reconciler of opposites:
earth and air, light and darkness, flesh and spirit—
returned at last, as in the prophecy,
in his manifestation as a bearded white man,
to end a greedy, destructive, blood-drunk age
of savagery, and usher in some new
era of global peace and harmony.

And even as I smile at the idea
of this balding, middle-aged, junior-high teacher-poet,
with four remaindered slim volumes clogging my basement,
as conqueror or redeemer of *anything,*
I'm thinking: well, why not? Maybe it's not so crazy.
If a savior were to appear or return today,
why not as a shy, romantic, lyric poet
out of phase with his time, but heralding another
with the slighted strength of quiet empathy
for leaves and stars and the invisible
connecting forces that flow all around and within us?

3

beyond the tangible, evanescent
present, the catchy popular song
on the jukebox, the cherry popsicle
on the steps of the museum, melting, fading
with cathedrals, pyramids, back to nothingness
in a seemingly godless world, without obvious purpose

some sense of transcendence, rising: mysterious
moments of wonder—sometimes the way the light
graces a cup, a mountain peak, lake, branch, shell,
or a face or a flower brushes you
with such beauty you feel yourself suddenly
welling, opening, flowing into some other
radiant, timeless unity...

4

Lord of Dawn, glimmering
Morning and Evening Star,
bridge between light and darkness,
is it you? Is it really you
who has risen out of the east
and come gliding over the sea on a floating hill
in this, the prophesied year of your return,
to claim again what was yours in ancient times?

O may it be so!
I, Moctezuma, ruler of Tenochtitlan,
emperor of all the land to both seas,
high priest of Huitzilopoctli, greedy Sun God—
preeminent in our times—but guardian still,
in my heart, of your quiet grace and modest wisdom,
pray it is you, Quetzalcoatl, come home at last
as I prepare to welcome
the tall, pale, bearded figure
approaching, a few minutes march
from the causeway to our city.

Creator of the sweet arts of civilization,
since your departure so long ago
the people have forgotten
your gentle ways, your selfless lessons
in how to elevate our sinful flesh,
the true, deep meaning of your sacrifice
when you cast yourself into the flames of a funeral pyre,
suffered torment in the underworld,
and rose again, purified, as the Morning Star.

What once was rich gesture, symbolic rite,
has turned into wholesale slaughter.

It is insane!
War in the name of religion,
religion war's insatiable prostitute!
Where, before, one honored volunteer
would mount, his heart aspiring higher and higher
with every step toward the waiting altar stone,
to give himself in ultimate sacrifice,
heart's blood returned to the sun who gives us life—
now thousands, taken in battle, are hauled up, bound,
screaming, chests slashed, hearts ripped out, raised,
still pulsing,
to the sky, then burned in the Sun God's honor,
heads and limbs hacked off, tossed
bouncing and slithering down the stinking stairs
blackened with rivers of blood.

O come now! It is time!
Feathered snake, balancing within yourself
the warring elements of flesh and spirit,
let your healing wings spread, rise, brightly hover
over this sick, dark age of humankind
so rich in gold and jewels, in pride and power,
but starved in spirit, compassion, true happiness.
We have marked the recent portents
of coming change:
the lake that surrounds our city suddenly
boiling, frothed with rage;
temples destroyed by lightning; the fiery comet
that rose and hung in the sky from midnight 'til dawn
like a flaming ear of corn.

But is it truly you
who even now I can see in the distance
like the head of some slowly uncoiling, monstrous serpent
as you ride along the causeway

leading your men on their strange, tall deer?
Let it be you, I pray, and not some foreign
gold-crazed adventurer or alien god
coming to smash our temples and build his own
with brick of our bones and blood.

I've listened with shock, misgiving,
growing terror,
to the rumors, reports
of the magical thundersticks your warriors carry
slung on their shoulders
that have struck down our neighbors
who dared to oppose you,
and the iron clothing that I myself can see
gleaming in sunlight as you turn
and, laughing, shout to your men,
that seems so unlike you.

O gentle savior, how can it be you
who has returned,
for the great disks of fine-wrought gold and silver,
the neckbands of precious green feathers and gems,
the mirrors and crowns and other treasures I sent you,
this one rusty helmet,
battered, rank with sweat,
that I've filled with gold nuggets, at your command,
and hold now in trembling hands as I descend
and walk toward the city's opening gates to greet you?

5

from the fountained courtyard
of our Hotel de Cortes
the sound each morning of sweeping,
splashing, sweeping—
relentless, insistent

scrubbing at the crust
of centuries' grime

the parrot in its cage
clutching the rusty padlock
with one claw
and tonguing, tonguing the keyhole

the *Mexico City News,*
which we try to avoid,
headlining the sickness of the present
most powerful leader in the world:
his new cancer, chronic
unslakable thirst for arms

some rhythmic, metallic
pulsing from the city
that suddenly stops

the beautiful girl
in the Metro, nursing a baby
swaddled in her rebozo:
Madonna in sneakers and plaid skirt

the hole in the wall I found
off the market in Patzcuaro—
the only place open at 7 a.m.—
where two wrinkled women,
busy with bean stew in a huge frying pan,
welcome me, smiling,
day after day,
bringing a large, clear glass
of steaming milk, Nescafe, sugar,
as if to say,"Write,
write, write! Whatever it is,
it must be important."

6

the heart, then, welling, burning
to give itself
to some other, greater
urgency, design . . .

but to reconcile that
with its own dark thirst
for blood?

easy enough to imagine
the small self groping
beyond its meager bounds
to connect with some other
eager, trembling soul:
flinching, responding
blissfully twining, blending . . .

but to square that, here and now,
with the face turned away
on the pillow next to yours
in the ringing, widening darkness
after the rush of bitter words
that were finally loosed, and meant
and no gentle touch or pleading
can summon back?

the ache to envision some ideal
new age, dimly evolving
as, heart-in-heart, two-in-one,
we push on toward the obscure
realm of All-in-One

brushing the quick of others, feeling the shock
of difference, possibility,
asking shyly to learn, impatient to share
our local wisdoms, stories, names
for Jesus, Quetzalcoatl,
mingling, jostling, losing ourselves
going under, in darkness
furled, suspended, waiting

to rise again, somehow
lighter, more spacious, marvelling
at the vast, spreading blossom
of the universe, glowing
all around and within us, flesh suffused
with joy, love, flickering, feathered
in soft light, poised
between night and morning: dawn . . .

but to catch any glimmering of that
at the block party, popping peanuts, guzzling beer
back to back with the guy whose succession of Dobermans
has scared the shit out of you and your kids
for the past twelve years;
and the woman whose manicured lawn
is your own mutt's favorite,
who glares from her window, quotes the local leash law,
and has sicked the cops on you a number of times;
the Santa Clausy senior citizen
whose business was candy
who waves and beams and sings out neighborly greetings
whenever you pass
and sets poisoned raccoon and squirrel traps
that did in one of your cats;
and the new, honey-blond young mother
whose succulent legs

you've nibbled on and up, as she suns in her yard,
but turns out to have zit pocks, hard, blank eyes,
and speaks with a whiny twang
about little but clothes?

7

the osprey I spotted
the other day, a month after we got back,
circling the nearby pond
where I stop for a minute, mornings
on my way out,
lucky to see a kingfisher or heron
along with the gulls and mallards
that still manage, somehow, to survive
the filthy water, rapidly silting in...

but, this time, majestic, silver-black, soaring wings
that, as I watched, folded, dropped
like a spear, spike, driven
by some unseen hammer, shattered
the calm, reflecting trees and sky,
kept going, pierced, plunged, disappeared
for what seemed more than seconds,
hours, light-years, the turbulence settling back
above it—so that I thought
it's knocked itself out, is drowning,
holding my breath—and then
came breaking through
again, the other way, struggling, wrestling
the heavy liquid pouring from it, spread
tremendous pinions and slapped, slammed, thrashed
the surface in a frenzy
of climbing, lunging forward, slowly rose

clutching, dragging something
bright, big, flashing
fiery gold in the sun—
too huge and wildly flailing, it seemed,
not to be dropped, escape—
but rowing, heaving, lifting, rose and rose,
then circled broadly, several times,
as if it too couldn't quite believe its catch
or to let the fisting needles
quiet that shuddering agony in its grasp,
and, finally, found a branch and settled there
for what must happen next . . .

As I drove off, heart-stunned, lost
in wonder, horror
still diving, wrenching up, gasping, slick with blood,
I suddenly thought: well, so much for transcendence!
then: no, wait—maybe that's how it *has* to be:
to plunge from some lofty vision
into the rich, stained beauty of the world,
feeling the dark swarm over our heads,
fierce nails drive through flesh and bone,
struggling up again, if at all,
body-and-spirit locked, inseparable:
dazzled, ecstatic, dying
as we ascend.

Empty Nest Haiku

Empty nest. Psych! Let's
gag the phone, strip, gaze, dance! You
say, "Work. Fifties. No."

You say, "I love you
but not like some roused goddess.
That's how it is now."

You say, "No one can
fulfill all another's needs."
Our hearts cut like jewels?

Strange season of new
passions in my middle years.
You say, "Go and grow."

Sax every night. New
York, half the week, exploring
changes, loneliness.

Amsterdam Ave. Glazed
dogshit. Heartache. Tip gigs. Still
go for it happy.

Each day three million
potential tantric lovers.
Never so alone.

All right all you tough
city slickers—where's someone
with the guts to love?

Friends say, "Blow your horn,
write. Be cool. Shaktis will come
in butterfly swarms."

Drawn by my open
sweet, compassionate vibe, they
light, sip, rest, flit on.

Warsaw . . . Osaka . . .
Newton . . . converge, join hands, dance
in my bursting heart.

You say, "You are free
to go, grow, fulfill yourself."
They say, "You're married."

Friend? Big brother? Saint?
or dirty old man, too weak
to take more than thanks?

Half empty, half full.
Tricks of perspective. Bullshit!
Half anything sucks.

MWM
seeks F open to explore
unqualified love.

Suppose I did find
a soul-and-body mate . . . where
would home be Christmas?

The urge to run home
hug you, safe, plead for a kind
of love you don't feel.

That book on tantric
ecstasy, flesh merged with soul—
salvation or doom?

For you Earth's solid
foundation, labor, harvest.
For me Heaven, Hell.

No sex without soul—
a resolve I shall live by.
Your health, my left hand.

If I did get in
some other's soul and pants, would
the foundation crack?

Nirvana, please . . . but
new in-laws, mortgage, Huggies
all over again?

So settle for art,
friends, ease back into comfy
safe once-a-moon sex?

Gently, slowly, could
I wake the goddess in you?
Or is she pure myth?

Checking back with you
about this one, that one, to see
if you'll crack or flip.

Asking permission
of Mommy? Or consulting
with an old, true friend?

Infantile ache to
curl back into the womb? Or
stretch out to the stars?

Foundation. Base camp
from which to go exploring
peaks shrouded in cloud.

Terrified? You bet.
Poised, teetering dizzily
at the crater's rim.

Lava of desire
seething, shouldering up to
connect with the sky.

To enfold the new
without crushing the old—love's
cramped "infinite pie"?

Big Bang. Infinite
expansion, all ways at once.
No point not center.

Back, forth, back, forth, New
York, Boston, where am I from?
Where am I going?

The guts to accept
it all, contradictions, say
here, this is me now.

Each morning get up
stretch my bones, spirit, head out
into the unknown.

Each night exhausted,
goddess fantasies, rising,
sinking down, down, down . . .

Keep open, moving.
To each new beauty, terror
yes, keep saying yes!

Such wasted beauties
tell me such sorrowful things
I start to hate men.

Shiva-Shakti? Shit!
For now talk, cappucino,
dance shy fingers, eyes.

Still, before I die
to connect, merge, let go, feel
stars swarm in my cells.

I say, "I love you
but search for Shakti elsewhere.
If I should find her . . . ?"

Shadow Haiku

We meet, peer across
darkness, light years, between stars.
Our shadows touch. Home.

Discussing weather
we feel the molten slither
of shadow glow. Joy.

Climbing the mountain
we stand gazing down to where
our shadows embrace.

One arm around me
the other shielding your heart.
Our shadows mock: "Hug?"

I say, "Your husband."
You say, "Your wife and two kids."
Our shadows say, "Hi!"

We analyze gaps
of age, culture, aura, sex.
Our shadows hold hands.

I cringe from your dark.
You squirm from my light's caress.
Our shadows shout, "Fools!"

You throw a pillow
and stamp. I reach for my coat.
Our shadows giggle.

I stare at the ground.
You look past me at the sky.
Our shadows soul-gaze.

We say, "I love you
but, but, but, but, but, but, but . . . "
Our shadows laugh, weep.

Halfway up, we slow
stop, dizzy, panting, glance back.
Our shadows turn, wait.

You snap shut your heart.
I stagger, adjust, back off.
Our shadows make bets.

"Too busy tonight."
We hang up. Our shadows swap
stories, dreams, 'til dawn.

I bus to New York.
You fly to San Francisco.
Our shadows lengthen.

We evolve, move on.
New jobs, friends, cafe partners.
Our shadows sit tight.

We return, smile, glad
everything's cool, in control.
Our shadows panic.

For weeks long wordless
messages on our machines.
Our shadows cocoon.

Blizzard. "You OK?"
"Yes . . . you?" "Yes." Silence screams, "Help!"
Our shadows spread wings.

We accept the bond,
dare Fate to whisper its name.
Our shadows listen . . .

"He softens her dark.
She deepens his light—each each
other's shadow guide.

"Falling in rapture
is one thing—love another."
Our shadows shrink . . . grow.

Near the mountain top
we tread air, slip, start to fall . . .
Our shadows catch us.

Heads brushing the sky
we balance, weave hands, light, dark—
one with our shadows.

Skipping Sex

"Let's skip sex,"
she says.
"It always gets so messy,
and I can tell it's already started
to cloud and sour and confuse
what has been such a beautiful
energy between us."

"Fine," I say—
"your choice.
As I've told you all along,
sex, for me,
is not what we're about
so much as the quiet
timeless, floating bliss
of being close
and feeling loved and safe."

"I can't decide about kissing,"
she says, after a while.

"I know," I say. "Kissing's tricky.
Maybe with lips clamped shut
would be OK?"

"I like that," she says.
"And hugging's allowed, but only
in a friendly sort of way."

"That's good," I say.
"Just like we're doing now."

"Exactly," she says.

"And gentle touching . . . confined
to . . . let's see . . .
head, and neck, and back . . . and arms."

"Sounds good to me," I say.

We lie there, skipping sex.

"But how," I wonder aloud
(after a timeless stretch
of friendly hugging
and a closed-mouth kiss or two)
"can I manage to dim the glow
that spreads like trickling honey
down into my belly
and the dark, fiery region
seething, just below
whenever we're holding hands?"

"I don't know," she says.

"It might be easier," I say,
"if you could avoid
those quick little jumpy squeezes
when our fingers are intertwined,
and those feathery circles
of deliciousness
you trace with satin tips
inside my palm."

"OK, I'll try
to remember that," she says.

"And when you laugh," I say,
"at some teasing idiocy of mine,
if you could just turn away

or use one hand to hide
that flash of ivory
and slithering pink,
I think I'd feel less lost
at the edge of some jungle
that scares me so, dares me
to enter and explore
until I drop and die."

"I see," she says.

"And those warm, pungent clouds
of seabreeze and rose and roots
that spice your breath
and snake up my nostrils
to attack my brain,
each puff a sweet, cruel death—
maybe a stick of spearmint gum
would help?"

"And your eyes," I continue,
breaking her wary silence—
"you could keep some shades
in a coat pocket . . . or here—
I'll get you a pair
of the ugliest ones I can find."

"Oh come on!" she laughs—
neglecting to turn, or hide
that prospect of savage lushness
that makes me collapse inside—
and gives me a playful slap.

"And when you call," I say,
stroking the sudden swarms
of blood invading my cheek,
"to give me my daily fix
of the various tints and flavors
trials and twists
your life's gone through
since we were last in touch,
or to detail, hour by hour,
your cluttered schedule
that makes it clearly impossible
to fit me in that day—
or when you're here, like this,
and tell me, for the third time,
you have to go,
I think it would ease
the unspoken tension significantly
if you could somehow, please—
if it's not beyond your choice—
remove those rustling silk ribbons
of mucus from your voice."

Butterfly Haiku

The silk butterflies
you gave me have escaped. Soft
knocking at my heart.

The fear love won't come
again, wings sweeping the sky.
The fear that it will.

Then God caught a flake
of sunlight, added a drop
of blood, and said, "Fly!"

Across a stormy
sea of doubt, fear, confusion—
hope's brave, foolish wings.

Coffee. Your half smile
heavy. My kind, tired eyes.
Sweet sips, wings resting.

My hand lights on yours,
flits off, returns, settles.
Yours opens: moist, dark, warm.

From pain's chrysalis
wings stretching, so delicate
Heaven would shred them.

Sun. Air. Talk. Laughter.
Lids pulse, flutter. Suddenly
trees shrink beneath us.

Love spreads out one wing
of passion, one of friendship.
Flying is balance.

Snow Haiku

Snow. Edges soften.
As we walk the city fills
with cherry blossoms.

Tired? Feet too cold?
we ask each other, walk on:
two snowflakes in wind.

Each flake is unique.
Our smiling eyes different
nights of the same moon.

Snow all day. You move
around the kitchen, singing
sweet slices of sun.

Snow drifts in my beard,
leaves flame, fall, through your voice—rich
beauty of ruins.

God's masterpiece: Death.
From flowers, fruits, leaf storms, snow
release, endless peace.

Joy. Again. Surprise!
Blooming from autumn's sorrow
winter's white wasteland.

Angel

A woman sits at the table next to mine
reading, alone, like me.
Two strangers, minding our own business,
resolved not to violate
what we sense are each other's
fragile, mending boundaries,
we are completely in love.

From the edge of one eye
I can see her head bent over her book
her face obscured by her arm
and cradling hand, one finger
winding tight, then letting slip
a lock of hair, over and over.

I do not turn when she looks up
to stare straight ahead
at what might have been,
drags on a cigarette, lifts her cold cup.

I know if I looked
the nose, too blunt or brittle,
the worn, chipped earshell,
the trace of an old scar
slicing the cheek,
or the overripe, bruised, or bitter
fruit of the mouth would confuse me.

I want her face to stay as it is now
flawless, so softly lit by grace
compassion, tenderness, desire, its revelation
would be too much to bear.

She does not look at me
for the same reason.

We are so happy
to have found each other at last
again, and this time
agreed not to meet,
not to let our eyes and voices
begin to explore one another
our bodies let go, embrace, with a deep moan
between agony and bliss, as our souls slide
through clothes and skin and terror
into each other,
acknowledging, with a ruby shiver
that we are going to be lovers,
that this, if the world keeps out of our way,
could be It.

We go on reading
letting the gentle shimmer
of the presence beside us
comfort and soothe and heal
our aching grief
for a vision dragged down in midflight
by the battered heart's failure
of faith and courage
over and over again

relieved to be holding each other
safely, at arm's length, eyes cast down,
two strangers in love completely
with the perfect being between us
resting its wings.

Little Doug

(poem on my 55th birthday)

"Mommy . . . Mommy . . .
Mommy . . . Daddy . . .
Mommy . . . "

A small, far voice
faint odor of paper-white
lilies, marzipan, salt . . .

"Mommy . . . Daddy . . . Mommy . . .
my eggs lake, the peeling
is ceiling monsters, a liger
at the bed of my edge, wings buzzbuzz
up my noses and ear . . . oh Dommy,
Maddy, the dark
too deep, moon poking
its lemon chickenfoot
hop, hop, hop, up my blanky, I'm all alone
drowning, drowning in jellystars . . . "

I press my ear
to the echoing shell inside me
and listen, breathing through cracks
the perfumed terror, fathomless aching
need.

The voice comes closer: "Don't leave me,
Mommy, the coats on hooks in the hall
are whispering scary things, the teacher
smells bony—where are you glowing? No, Mommy!
I want to go with you . . . don't o aglay!

"Mommy, the ocean won't stop
hissing and leaping and crashing, the Bandycramps
talk funny yahyah, spit clicks, laughing, swinging
me into the icy way graves, icy slicing
my legs and tummy, stabbing my eyes, laughing, laughing
and clissing, yahyah . . . Don't make me stay here, please,
Mommy,
come take me home.

"Curled tight on the top bunk I won't
fall awake if I stay off
moaning all night, Mr. Mad Flashlight
Eye says, 'Shut up and go to sleep, go to sleep,
so to gleep.' Curled tight I won't . . . every morning
in the mushy woods, whistling, cackling, I fall
behind, stumbling, my knees . . . owww! Daddy,
wormrogsnakeslime all over me,
blicking my lud, I know
you're ashamed to me, Maddy, but but
the others are shoulder, jigger, Dommy, I'm only
five fears old, oh please, please
let me hum comb . . .

"And Mommy, if Daddy's there, this time please
don't cry and moan,
dreaming at Scaddy, and Daddy don't
talk so soft, I can't—louder, tell Mommy
'I love you, Mommy, I love you,' and hold Mommy
tight in your arms, hug her, hugger, hugger
so close she can't woan and mail, and stroke her
pretty soft hair, gently, gently, and kiss her, I would
if I wasn't so little and flaking
under a lizard of spankies, oh Tummy
my mommy aches!

"Mommy, please stop now, listen,
yes, listen, remember
that sunny sweet summer
smell of hay in the barn, purply pigeons
cooing in honey gold rafters, green fields and meadows
blossoming rubies and sapphires, sparkling cold streams
we splashed and shrieked in, stuck dragonflies
glistening in air, huge yellow and blue-green
tolloswales flittering off as we chased them
through jack-in-the-grasshoppers, tripped and fell splat
in the warm sweet long grass and lay laughing
and rolling together, crawling to look
for over a four-leaf clovers . . . cool lime
evenings, porch cots, fireflies, Mikey and me
farting and snorting 'til Daddy came out
and said, 'Enough now,' and sometimes, sometimes
sat down and made up a story, his Lucky Strike
fireflying in darkness, Tony Avocado
who lived in the bathtub drain and had such
magic adventures, then flew back
and shrank back down into the drain . . . drifting off in the avocado-eyed
hoohooing darkness . . . fresh mornings of cream
and strawberry jammountains, all of us sitting together,
joking and plans and punny, you butter
go bacon a beach, eggsactly, the ponies just like in books only
smelling much stronger, the giant-wheeled tractor
jiggling and bumping us all the way
to heaven and back, pink cow balloons spurting
and foaming in silver buckets, and everything
flowing and shining, don't start again, Mommy,
I'll hug you, take care of you, Mommy, it's all right, oh
Dommy, Dommy, don't you remember that farm?"

Cycle

Chipped slivers of light
slip all around me,
spin down to meet,
become their shadows.

Another harvest
of hopes and dreams
that greened and spread,
turning themselves to the sun,
drunk on sweet rain,
high on hot streams of gold,
flourished or failed,
drained now, exhausted, let go . . .

Another crop
of terrors, pains
straining to bear up
battered by gusts and storms
hanging on, twisted,
whirl now, curled, dizzily down . . .

'til the ground is a maze
of scattered trash and treasure—
rose, ocre, scarlet,
topaz, garnet, mauve,
glad for release, rustling faintly, waiting
for frost's cold calm shield.

While naked trees
shiver skeletons, creak
and nod,

drifting into a blank
dream of endless rest,
muffled, snug in snow . . .

until the first
needles of green
prickle that numbness, pierce
and prod them from sleep
to stir, stretch
bleed and bloom
with anguish and joy, again.

A Purple Rose

(for Pat)

No one before ever gave me
a purple rose
out of the blue
from the depths of night
to bathe my bleary eyes
at the bathroom mirror
with fresh delight
and spread that sweet
tingly feeling
from crown to toes
of how special I must be
just being me.

No one before
ever crinkled up her nose
smiling sunbeams at me
despite warnings of wrinkles
to let me know, over and over,
that I am the star
of her heart's favorite show.

No one before ever answered
my call to come out and play
in the green-gold meadows
of Wonder Childhood,
wandering, timeless
together through the Now
of beebells and clover
butterdreams, rainbow streams,
flopping to wallow
and whisper, with giggles and shrieks,

to the smiles of Father Sky and Mother Earth
in the warm fields of Yes.

No one before ever lay with me all morning
naked, belly to belly, mouth to mouth
without thinking it must be time
to turn away to more important things—
the news, piling bills, the phone,
brushing their shrill urgency aside
for some future Now,
stroking, soothing the marrow-ache
of a frightened child,
cries echoing through the dark
of half-a-century,
pouring her healing light
into that pit of terror, rage, and shame
that I labor each day, alone
to fill with self-fathering love
but cannot learn
to share, risk giving, receiving
despite fears of sudden emptiness or drowning
on my own.

No one before ever dared
to open and let me in
to the ghost-webbed, murky rooms
of old abandonments,
early, guilt-choked entanglements,
in caves where nightmares flutter,
cling and swoop,
to let me touch the quick
and gently kiss and lick
that quivering, wounded core
of birthright pleasures.

No one before ever followed, on and on,
the snarled twists and turns
of hopes, doubts, visions, fears
that maze my head,
spinning out, interweaving
her own with mine
as we search for some glimmering
thread of Truth
to live by, extend, and grow,
while around our laced fingers, dreams
the sun climbs and sinks
behind porch, or bay, or leaves,
or the dark at the window softens
into dawn, and we laugh, groan, sleep.

No one before ever woke me
with tongue thrusting through my lips
or snailing my ear,
hands roaming, exploring, unashamed, everywhere,
rousing my sleepy desire
with wave after wave of tender
ecstasy, sweeping my flesh
'til I let go, in bliss, surrender,
or swelling, rise and shed
my pallid skin,
a green god emerging, turning
to greet his long-searched-for soul-mate
mother, sister, Earth goddess
blurred into one,
my cock-flute throbbing,
calling her into the ageless dance
of scepter and lotus,
breast chalice, sacred fount,
passion cresting and frothing

as we plunge and play
fins flashing, souls slipping in and out
of depths and currents, blue-green
ocean eyes.

No one before ever gave me
this feeling of being
so tremblingly alive,
at fifty-five growing,
delicate, vulnerable, bruised, newborn, exposed—
rich inner petals unfolding:
a purple rose.

Wallowing

"Know what's funny?"

"What?"

"My knee hurts."

"Really?"

"Yep."

"Huh. And know what?"

"What?"

"Mine's stopped."

"Yeah, well . . . figures."

"Which one?"

We look from the pillow
at the snowy tangle
of knobs bulging the sheet.

"I can't tell," she says, laughing.

We give up, snuggling closer
letting slip all sense
of whose is which what.

Valentine

(for Pat, February 14, 1996)

Because we still refuse
to give up our right
to believe we deserve
to love and be loved,
be nurtured and nurture
heart, body, mind, and soul

despite the dim path ahead
bristling with childhood monsters
snarling, crouched to spring,
but lonely, perhaps, also, longing
for welcoming arms, forgiveness, gentle stroking,
to be set free to sprawl in sunlight
and go their ways
or pad along as our guides

and despite the deep pits behind us,
littered with rusty armor
shards of dreams,
we have crawled from, bleeding
fragile, slowly mending,
hoping our tears
will heal and keep the scars
of loss, rage, guilt, fear, sorrow
from closing us off for good,

we turn to each other
here and now
with hope and choice and courage
steadying our hands,
praying this time we will learn

to be strong enough to be tender,
brave enough to surrender
open to trust, let go
melting, giving, taking in
the miracle of each other,
as we plunge together
into the unknown
of each new day's
endless flux and flow.

Exploring

(for Val, in memoriam
and Pat, in the now)

1

We never found what we were looking for:
a stretch of leafy woods, a quiet
path we could explore
for an hour or two that late May afternoon
soaking in green, freshening with clear song
heads bleared and achy
from the drive half-way home across the state
after the morning's burial—
a walk before returning to the inn
to flop on the big bed, snuggle, flow with the lazy
late sunlight creeping across the ceiling and walls,
then wash up, come down for a relaxing drink
at the six-stooled Pub and Bar
and try to let go, ease down, and settle in
to a place we'd never been before.

The woods were guarded by no parking signs,
the lakes by fences, dirt roads marked Beware!
visions of Eden blocked by glinting barrels
of local shotguns, pick-ups taking the curves
of narrow roads like bad-assed bats out of Hell.
We smiled, a bit tensely, said, "Well, we're exploring—"
having rejected the too-familiar spots
of candle-lit inns and well-marked trails
alive on weekends with peace-seeking city folk,

chipmonks, warblers, and ghosts of former times –
"and exploring's just that: you don't know what you'll find."
What we'd found was country, small towns geared for work,
privacy, weekend turkey hunts and fishing,
and that the curves and edges of our need
would not fit the puzzle of this posted landscape.

2

Giving up the walk, we pulled in at Travels End
that had the inviting look
of an old weathered tavern with some local tradition
in the village next to ours
with its gas station, pizza place, drug and general store—
but whatever it once was had been turned, inside
into a glossy, modern Italian restaurant,
the small bar crammed and nobody in a hurry.

We poked in at some neoned bar and grill
loud with TV's and blank-mouthed stares,
withdrew, and drove on to our inn
the guide book said was homey with nearby lakes.

3

Six-thirty when we arrived, tired and hungry,
we skipped our snuggle and laze
and had the mini pub-bar to ourselves,
sipping and taking in the local news
from the chatty owner and young waitresses
one of whose boyfriend had left a message
twenty minutes before, reporting some "small emergency"
involving their son—but when she'd called back
there'd been no answer. We offered our concern,

half-logical hopeful reassurances
to her jittery confusion, not daring to leave
in case he called from somewhere else
while she was on her way home.

Dewar's and Merlot seeping through the strain
of the day—my big sister's urn-globed ashes
sinking into a gouged dark cube of space
beneath a chiseled upright stone proclaiming
"And death shall have no dominion."
"Right!" I'd thought, chanting alien psalms and phrases
about sin and Hell and eternal resurrection,
still wobbly from the five-hour drive from Boston
the night before, through downpours, overtaking
hissing, red-eyed hundred-wheelers—with flashes of Val
from photos and dusty crevices in my brain:
introducing me, when I was in junior high
and she in college, to the riches of Hopkins and Thomas,
and encouraging my early fumbling attempts
at poetry; sitting side by side in chairs
in her dorm room, guiding me through the obscure logistics
of reaching across the darkened empty space
of a movie house to take a girl's sweaty hand
into one's clammy own—
while your sleepy, insistent sense,
gazing out at the streaming black,
that we were on some strange highway above clouds
floating below us over hidden valleys,
grew more and more surreal as fatigue set in,
and the thought of the family gathering next morning—
the sad, familiar faces, brave and bruised,
I'd somehow have to find words for
as we hugged and chatted, skimming

for an hour or two our complex, uncertain lives—
seemed increasingly beyond
what I, Welbutrin, and Ativan could handle.

4

Our dinner was an unexpected treat!
Wine and Scotch blunting the edges
of the day's anxieties, the unknowable future,
we eased and opened, talked about life and death,
despair and hope, the need people have for each other—
though they rarely dare to admit it—
life's weave of happiness, suffering . . . and a kind
of hazy, welling joy began to shimmer
as we communed and shared, became two blending
interconnected parts of the same being,
opening, exploring, on and on
a dense inner landscape of hidden hurts and fears
wanting to come out, be heard and understood
in the healing light of acceptance and compassion:
the clinging ghosts of our childhood dreads
of abandonment or engulfment; current forebodings,
in our fifties, of ending up unloved, alone;
the collapse of my marriage, after twenty-five years,
my leaving, the relief, the aftershock
of guilt and grief, rage, terror, disbelief,
the added stress of beginning to work through
complexities of the upcoming divorce;
your courageous vulnerability, prying open
defenses to take on, give yourself, again
to the potential nightmare
of another still-married man . . .

Alone together, able to speak it all out,
take in and feel for one another—no prophets,
but, in the midst of the unknown, committed
to nurturing what we had established
over a year of living mostly together,
getting used to each others' compulsions, frailties, quirks
we each feared would push the other's panic button,
and the latest wave of mingled joy, hope, fear
from my giving up my apartment
and moving in with you—the deepened sense
of acceptance, safety . . . the pangs of heightened risk.
Admitting it all, we held hands, smiled, and drank
to going for it, one day at a time,
doing our best to give love and support
to each other, whatever challenges might come up,
reaffirming our on-going mutual desire
for evolving, open, intimate, soul-body love.

5

We rose from the table different from when we'd sat,
tipped the waitress overgenerously, went out
into the glimmering evening, and found the walk
that had eluded us all afternoon
because of our too rigid image,
right by the inn: a wooden bridge, lilacs, a brook
swirling with new, winged life; then a little road
we climbed where a mother and kids were playing
with a soccer ball I rescued at one point
from disappearing downward into the dark.
We exchanged friendly greetings and strolled on,
hand-in-hand, checking out the half-lit houses,
looking down sideyards to the dusky lake,
feeling that we were family among family,

part of the whole global family, at risk,
all needing each others' love and nurturing;
and as I recalled the morning: tears and hugs
and heartfelt words and eyes brimmed with compassion,
I thought, well, maybe death really has no dominion
as each loving, kind, compassionate word or act
goes rippling on forever, coming out
again and again—as Val's encouraging help
was still at work in my poetry forty years later,
still nudging my hand to reach across dark space
and lace with yours, despite the risks, so glad
we'd found each other, were here together, pausing
to kiss or look at this and that—in no hurry
to get anywhere beyond the blissful moment
of where we were, here and now, gently linked together,
having found what we were really looking for
in a place we never would have thought to find it,
by just being, going on, through disappointment
at the fenced-off old, into the cloudy new,
not pushing, letting it be and evolve
in its own time, whatever way it would,
moving on, together, two separate, blended beings
at peace now, bathed in the quiet grace of love.

May, 1996

Anniversary

(for Pat, July, 1996)

You say I'm the love of your life,
at 56, the best thing
that's ever happened to you.

How I long
to say the same things back to you
so simply,
but can't, yet, tangled, torn . . .

though I often feel them
in one of those clearings
of birdsong and flowering
Peace, Hope, Love, and Joy
I come upon
as I make my obscure way
from the old to the new

through forests of Grief
seething crators of Rage
rose-covered pits of Might Have Been
snares of Guilt
trecherous bogs of Anxiety and Depression
where I falter, collapse, exhausted
lie overwhelmed, helpless, for hours, eternity,
letting go, drifting, sinking, struggling up
to wrestle some looming phantom
from childhood: Neediness or Dependency
that I embrace with one arm
while pushing it back with dread,
or one of the Terror Twins: Abandonment and Engulfment,
or take on that gang of contemporary ogres:

Uprootedness, Dislocation, Readjustment,
Uncertain Finances, Upcoming Divorce—

having moved, this past year
from a twenty-six-year-old marriage
of diverging paths and fraying connections,
for a dream of evolving, intimate, soul-body love,
to an unfamiliar place I called my own,
then to your place, and now, setting out together,
to a new place of our own
where the half-filled rooms still have trouble
remembering where and what they are.

I say you're the only one
I know or can imagine
with the patience and compassion
to let me go through all this
as I try, in my fifties,
to heal and grow,
and reassure me, when I need it,
that I'm not letting you down
or proving too weak
for what you want in a love-partner for life,

having been where I am
a number of times yourself
raked by thorns, sweat-drenched, trekking the wilderness
of some recent devastation
that stirs up, blurs
with a shadowy nightmare world
of famished, wailing
earlier deprivations
that such as you and I
must journey back to
confront and lock with

again and again—
phantasmagorical fangs and claws—
'til we drop, or they slack their crippling grip
and we slip through
to the sunsweet fragrances
of Understanding, Acceptance, Compassion, Forgiveness
in the meadow of Loving Oneself
which leads out to the land of Loving Others.

You are the only one
open and brave enough
to intermingle intimacies with me
in a flow of trust and acceptance, letting out
clenched silent weepings, streaming secret wounds,
offering words of wisdom or consolation
to make it better, soothe the ache away,
or just an ear, a nod, a sigh
a hand gently stroking shoulder, neck, or back
letting the other know they're not alone.

The only one
who delights in surprising me
and being surprised
by little somethings:
a stone, a shell, a flower from the yard,
a card for no special occasion
in the fridge,
that makes no dent in the pocket of the giver
but brims the receiver's heart
with priceless joy.

The only one
who'll sit beside me, clang the locking bar
and ride the gut-churning, sanity-defying
ups and downs, sickening curves,

tumbling passions, rising ecstasies, terrors, bursts
of laughter, swerves of doubt, relief, as we go
wherever it is we're going
side by side.

All of which is my long way 'round
of getting to where you stand
smiling, waiting patiently for me
to say, as I do now,
that you are the love
whose tender, cradling, passionate embrace
deep, lingering gaze and kiss,
overflowing heart and open need for me
I've dreamed of, wakened in anguish without
for half-a-century,
the most intense, scary, wonderful thing
that's ever happened to me.

Nights

We take turns
listening to each other
snore

sleepless
from stress, or chemicals
exploring

anti-anxiety
anti-depression
antacid—one, or two more?

lulled, jarred
by the rhythmic
release, and building
gravelly nasal roar.

Half of us is sleeping
heavily, drifting, naked
through the night

while the other half
keeps watch, counting heartbeats
owling the dark

for old demons, ghostly monsters—
shushing them, fiercely
shooing them away.

Half of us is sleeping,
healing . . . soon
it will be day.

Valentine II

(for Pat, February 14, 1997)

A year later
still walking hand-in-hand
the darkening, brightening path
from the Old to the New
through the Forest of Love,

past Terrors, Sorrows,
Guilts, Shames, Doubts
still lurking, stalking us
leaping out snarling!

Shaking, we kneel, croon
soothing spells and chants,
holding out handfuls of sweet
Welcome, Compassion, Encouragement
Hopes and Dreams.

Astonished, they pause,
stunned, sniff and lick—
their clouded eyes wrestling
with ancient hungers, whips;
softening, trembling
as they nuzzle our fingers
a bit longer each time
before dashing away,

wanting to trust, beginning
to almost believe
their grizzled hearts
could heal, laugh, learn to play.

Legacy

(for Pat)

1

Of course you are my mother
and I your father—
here, as you cradle me nuzzling at your breast
and I shelter you, nestled, burrowing in my arms—
giving each other, as best we can
what we've ached for so long
despite the whispers
of terror, guilt, and shame—
echoes from half-a-century ago
still chilling our hearts and creeping up our spines.

The warm, milky sweetness
of spreading bliss
I'd suck in one night,
curdled the next by sobs and moans and wails
flooding the stairs, sweeping under my door
up the crib, through the pillow over my head . . .

The strong, tender arms
and crooning voice
that wrapped you like angel wings
in cozy safety on Thursday,
empty and bitter by Friday midnight, reeking
of rage and unfulfillment,
lurching, slurred and leering
past your cracked door . . .

2

Too young, too scared, too helpless
to fathom or deal with inconsistent gods,
we'd huddle, cower, curl from the dim monsters
clawing the dark panes, spidering up the blanket
or grinning down in the nightlight
through cracks in the wallpaper flowers,
trembling, ashamed, believing that empty ache
was all that we deserved, unworthy
of being loved beyond the meager diet
we received—our desperate need for more
a selfish weakness . . .

and grew up afraid
to open, freely give and take and trust
heart's richness—sealed off
by layers of scars surrounding
a famished emptiness, a need too great
that tried to suck dry, scared away
many who tried to love us.

And still now, fifty years later,
as locked in each other's arms we sink to sleep,
we rouse and stir up phantoms that wail and hiss,
"No, no little one! The love you crave is poison.
Wrap yourself round with fear, and go well-armored
through a sweet-tongued, venomous world."—
and wake, sweat-drenched, uncertain where we are,
reaching out, through a fading gauze of ghosts
in terror the other will have turned to empty dark
or a gaping cauldron, seething
with hysterical pain, need, rage.

3

Nonetheless, somehow, we survived—
grew up, had lovers, jobs, spouses, kids, dinner parties—
and good grew out of it as we strove to nurture
happiness from those early sips of Eden,
through will and imagination wove a tight
more consistent love than we'd received . . .
and yet, underneath, that sense
of apprehension, rumbling unfulfillment
building, swelling, festering inside—
something rich and precious locked away
aching to burst forth, blossom or turn to ash
in ecstasy, or terror . . .

pills for anxiety, pills for depression
to blunt the edge of anguish and despair,
and, finally, disillusion, rage, refusal
to accept as life that smooth-surfaced routine
of work, news, drinks, books, closed-mouthed sex in the dark.

Searching, stumbling, desperate, at last we found
a place of courage from which to plunge
into the wilderness inside ourselves
and make the long trek back
to rusty gates, charred scales and scraps
of iridescent feathers,
familiar shadows moping outside the walls,
moaning and cursing, rattling the padlocked door,
and, swept by fury, we clutched their throats
and slammed their tattered shells
over and over to the dusty ground,
until, exhausted, weeping, we raised them up
and saw their torment and regret,
the impotent fear-grimed love streaking their faces,

their tortured incapacities,
shackled by their own childhood
demons and angels wrestling in the dark,
too twisted, terrified, crippled
to give more than they had to us,
and drew them, with compassion, tenderly
into our shivering arms, and wailed with them,
suffering together, stroking their ashen hair,
smoothing their faces, accepting them as they were,
releasing them, gently, beginning to forgive
the damage they'd done us, and slowly purge and heal
the shame and guilt and terror in ourselves.

4

So here we are, having found each other
in the midst of all this, through luck, or chance, or grace,
at fifty-five-and-six, snuggling like babies,
opening slowly, night after night,
blissfully, fearfully,
learning to hold each other
close, and closer, hearing each other out
as walls crack and the bitter flood gushes through—
not turning away, holding on, caressing each other
soothing fear and shame, soaking in peace and love,
both fumbling as we try to disentangle
sick strands of ancient shame, paralysing terror
from the skein of healthy needs, natural desires;
patient, together, committed to the years
of self-work and work together it will take
to dim the scary darkness, drive away
the lurking spiders, learn to risk and trust
the shelter of my arms, the balm of your breasts . . .

unfolding, playfully, touching, reclaiming
petal by petal, the legacy
that Nature had in store for us: delight
in all our senses, urging us on to explore
with joy and wonder each pleasure
in our own and each other's bodies,
and venture out, as if for the first time,
into the universe beyond,
drawn by each color, texture, song
to the fresh miracle, mysterious web
of stone and shell, leaf, wing, and hand and star . . .

finding again that hidden sunlit meadow
where a little boy lies gazing up
at a heavenly feast of bursting cherry blossoms,
and a little girl in a yellow dress floats by,
light and pure as a sunbeam, stops and giggles,
kneels down next to him,
and they lie, hands linked, and stretch and savor and bask
in the rich warmth spreading
inside, and all around them, simple as two
butterflies sipping nectar, brimmed
with gold as two buttercups,
green as two blades of grass.

Soulmates

(A Wedding Valentine for Pat, February 14, 1998)

You say "blue"
and I'm awash
in vast surges, sighs
of salty
eternally wounded, resilient
little-girl-woman's eyes.

I say "cool"
and your fingers
flick and snap
hips, shoulders sway
to the saxy
breath of galaxies
at play.

We say "love"
and Apollo's axle . . .
Venus, shimmery . . .
jump-starting Jupiter . . .
oh enough
of that slithery
life-approximating
poetic stuff . . .

Why not just say,
here on this most romantic
Valentine's wedding day,
we two are one!
Cliché . Half true. No fun!

OK, let's see, then . . . try
we one are two . . .
each says
we do!
we do!

An Ordinary Morning

You wake to the light
of an ordinary morning

but something about the way
it's reflecting, refracting, slightly
differently, as if reaching
into, beyond, the surfaces
of things more deeply, lovingly
reluctant to let them go . . .

and things themselves
(the warm, immaculate
sheet peeling back with your hand
to reveal a mysterious
castle at the edge of a darkly shining forest
in the midst of soft hills and valleys, honeyed plains
you recognize, but hardly knew were there)
more freshly aware, even reverently
what they always were, though blurring at the edges
and slipping in and out of each other's names
as at a party where everyone turns out
to be distantly related . . .

and suddenly, as you're pissing
a gold stream into an alabaster
chalice—you realize
that though it's the same old world
of heartbreak and politics, genocide, housework, pollution,
for the moment all that's been balanced, panned back from,
swept under
a fathomless surge of calm, grace, awe, love, joy . . .

and then, once you've squirmed back into your skin
and are strapping the day to your wrist
it hits you that you've arrived
at something that's beginning
to feel like a whole new way
of seeing things and being: a new age
of inextricably tangled fact and wonder
beautiful, terrible, beyond hope or despair,
that you must accept and try to celebrate
in its almost unbearable richness

though it seems to have little to do
with the quest you thought you were on
toward the solution to some definable problem,
and even as it begins may be nothing more
than a moment's frozen perspective
in which all that appears
to be constant, eternal, is really
heading off elsewhere, toward God knows what . . .
but by now you're up, dressed, ready
for almost anything.

Typeset in Granjon with Optima titles.
Book design by William L. Bauhan and Sarah F. Bauhan.
Printed by Thomson-shore, Dexter, Michigan